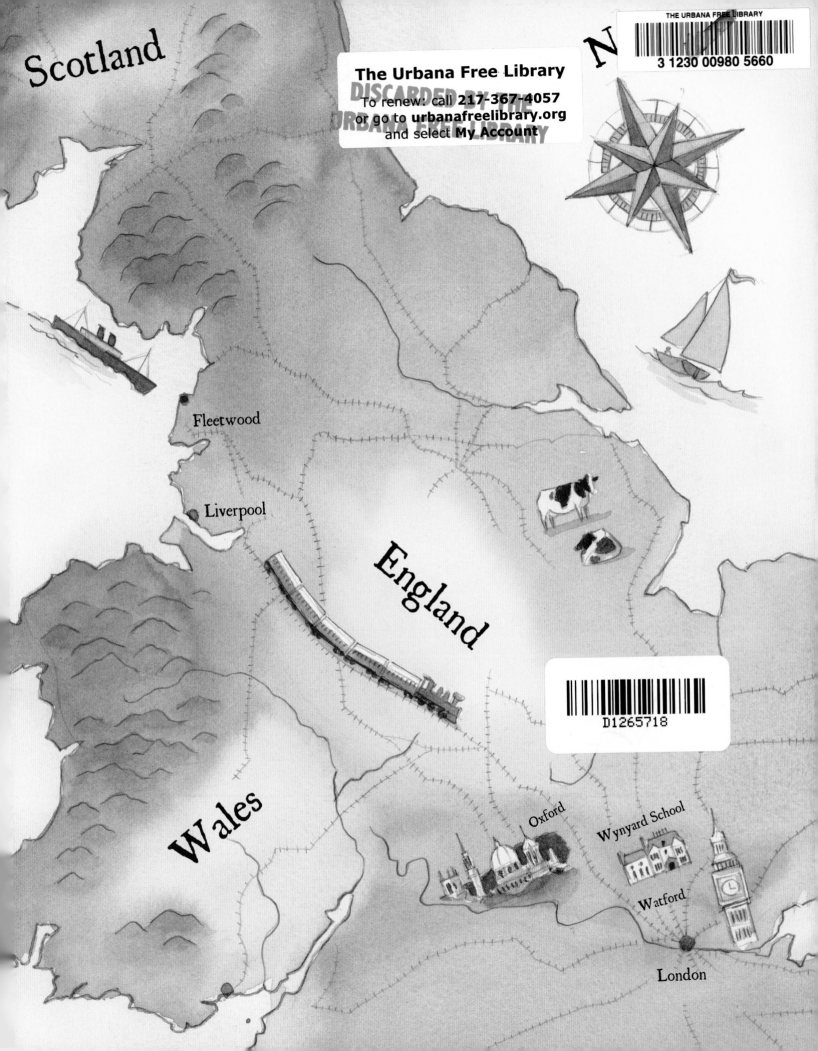

Scotland

N

Fleetwood

Liverpool

England

Wales

Oxford

Wynyard School

Watford

London

FINDING NARNIA

THE Story of C. S. Lewis and His Brother

Caroline McAlister

Illustrated by Jessica Lanan

Roaring Brook Press

New York

Jack and Warnie weren't just brothers; they were best friends. But they were very different. From the beginning, it was Jack who dreamed up stories of other worlds.

Warnie liked to sit in the wide picture window of their new house and watch the busy world of the Belfast shipyards. He could see teams of men hammering sheets of metal over the skeletons of huge ocean liners.

Jack preferred to look through the window of his imagination. He browsed the bookshelves that lined the walls. When he read about Balder the Brave, who was so bright that light could shine through him, the story was more real to him than any ocean liner.

Sometimes Warnie pretended to be an Indian raja.
He drew maps of railways with trains that crisscrossed
the vast Indian continent on a strict schedule.

4

Sometimes Jack pretended to be a brave knight.
He sketched a map of a dagger-shaped isle ruled by
a mouse king whose castle was under attack.

Once in a while, Warnie's raja would visit Jack's island and
help the knight defend the castle. And every now and then,

Jack's knight would visit the raja and ride a train through the Indian hill country. In spite of their differences, it was always fun to play together.

One rainy day, the brothers were exploring the long hall of the new house. In a little room next to the attic, full of hat boxes and steamer trunks, Jack found an old wardrobe. He turned the knob. The hinges creaked. He sputtered and coughed. The smell of moth balls made him gag.

But he burrowed behind the rough wool and tickly fur, anyway.
What if the wardrobe had no end, he wondered.
Warnie stayed outside. Perhaps he even warned Jack, "Don't shut
yourself in." The brothers always looked out for each other.

When Jack and Warnie's mother fell ill, the house was busy with doctors coming and going, and strange medicine smells wafted down the long hallways. Downstairs their father paced the big empty rooms. Upstairs Jack made his own imaginary world, and Warnie joined him. They called it Boxen.

Jack drew a map of Boxen's teeming capital city.
He sketched the parliament house, the stock
exchange, shipyards, a train station,
and a music hall.

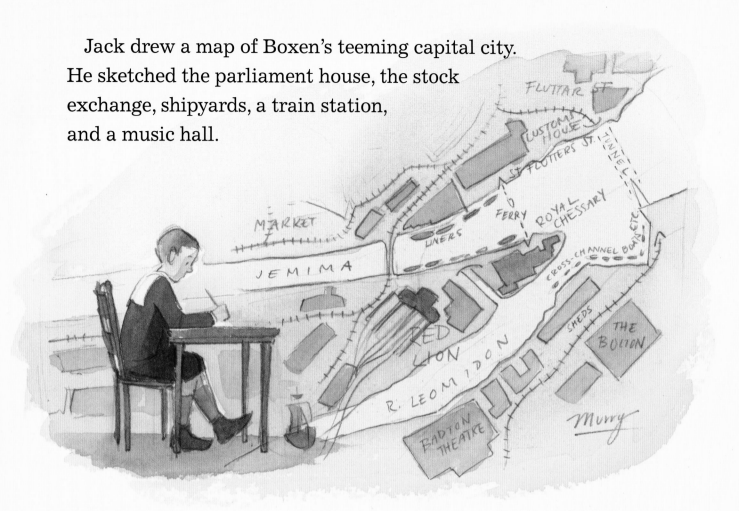

Warnie designed a steamship to travel from
Boxen to India and back. He included an
engine room, a telegraph, and an anchor winch.

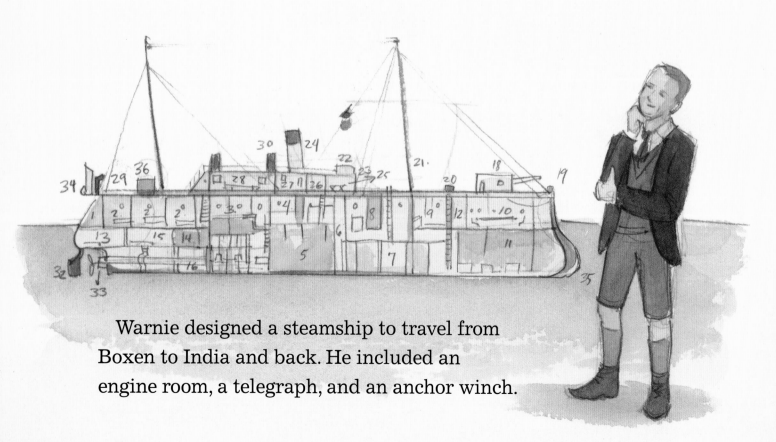

Jack wrote Boxen's newspaper, Warnie made Boxen's railroad schedule, and together they held a double coronation where Jack and Warnie wore their crowns and smiled and waved.

Day after day, as they played in the small room in the big, sad house, Jack wondered: What if they could escape to Boxen and stay there?

But when their mother died, their father sent Jack and Warnie away to boarding school. They dressed up in stiff Eton collars, awkward knickerbocker pants, and comical bowler hats, and

Jack hated the strange English accents and flat brown fields. He feared the headmaster with his thick beard and heavy cane. And he never got to read the stories he loved; instead, he worked on endless math problems. He longed for the holidays when he and Warnie could return to the attic and Boxen. Only then could Jack wonder what if . . .

Many years passed. The whole world went to war.

Separated in different regiments, Jack and Warnie worried about each other.

When the war ended, Jack became a teacher at Oxford. He was an important man who gave serious lectures and wrote long books. But sometimes he saw things through the window of his imagination.

Warnie continued to work for the army. Whether he was stationed in Colchester, Woolwich, or Shanghai, he sat behind a desk and typed forms— long forms and short forms, forms in black ink, and forms in red ink.

At long last, Warnie retired from the army and moved in with Jack. Once again, the two brothers lived together in a spacious house whose walls were lined with books. There was even a wardrobe, the same wardrobe from their old home in Ireland, where they used to pretend they were the princes of Boxen.

Another terrible war broke out. Families in London sent their children to the countryside to be safe from the bombs. On Sundays, Jack noticed the church was full of refugee children, squirming uncomfortably on unfamiliar pews among unfamiliar people. He didn't know much about children, but he figured he and Warnie could help out.

That's how two girls came to stay with Jack and Warnie. One rainy day, the girls were exploring the house, and they found the old wardrobe. They turned the door knob. The hinges creaked. They sputtered and coughed. The smell of moth balls made them gag.

The girls asked Jack, "What's on the other side?" The question opened a creaky door in Jack's mind. For the first time in a very long time he began to wonder what if . . .

Scritch scratch. He wrote and wrote. Every time he paused to dip his pen in ink, a new idea came to him. First the lamppost and faun came alive. Then two boys and two girls entered through a wardrobe.

Tip tap. Warnie deciphered Jack's inky scribbles
and typed a clean copy on his Royal typewriter.
The story reminded him of Boxen.

But the story wasn't about Boxen. That story
ended long ago.

This story was about a place called Narnia. Covered in snow, Narnia still glows with light from an enchanted lamppost. A faun with an umbrella steps from behind the trees.

A family of beavers waits in the bushes,

a white witch glides on a sled,

and a majestic lion watches them all.

Author's Note

"The other blessing was my brother. Though three years my senior, he never seemed to be an elder brother; we were allies, not to say confederates, from the first. Yet we were very different."

—C. S. Lewis, *Surprised by Joy*

Clive Staples Lewis and Warren Hamilton Lewis spent their early childhood in Belfast in Northern Ireland. When it was rainy they took refuge in a little room in the attic. At first, each created his own imaginary world. Jack (C. S. Lewis) called his Animal-Land; there were knights, castles, and talking animals dressed as humans. Warnie (W. H. Lewis) created his own version of Colonial India. Jack's fantasy world was literary, influenced by the legends he had read of medieval chivalry, while Warnie's was more realistic and technological, full of trains and boats. Eventually they merged the two worlds into one so that they could play together, naming the new land Boxen, allegedly because of the old boxes and trunks that filled the little room. And yes, there was a wardrobe. It was hand carved by their paternal grandfather in the 1800s.

In 1908, when Jack was nine and Warnie thirteen, their mother died from cancer, and her death profoundly altered what had been a very happy childhood. Their father sent the boys to Wynyard School, which C. S. Lewis referred to as Belsen in his autobiography. Shortly after Jack left, it shut down because of complaints about the headmaster's cruelty. Jack then spent two years at Malvern College, a boarding school Warnie had loved but Jack hated. In fact, their difference in opinion over the school was one of the only things that caused conflict between them. Before proceeding to the Royal Military College at Sandhurst for Warnie and Oxford University for Jack, both brothers studied privately with a tutor named W. T. Kirkpatrick. Jack named Professor Kirk in *The Lion, the Witch and the Wardrobe* after his tutor, whom he adored.

World War I interrupted Jack's studies at Oxford. He was wounded at the Battle of Arras. Warnie was stationed in France at the time and made a one-hundred-mile journey by bicycle to visit Jack in the hospital. After the war, Jack resumed his studies and eventually became a faculty member at Oxford, where he taught and wrote books about medieval and renaissance literature.

At Oxford, most of Jack's closest friends were Christians. In 1929, he began to believe in God and in 1931, after a long midnight ramble with Hugo Dyson and J. R. R. Tolkien, he became a practicing Christian himself. It was around this same time that Jack and J. R. R. Tolkien began meeting as the Inklings, an informal literary society that gathered at The Eagle and Child pub and read aloud from their works in progress.

Warnie continued to work for the army as an officer in charge of supplies. He spent time in far-flung posts, such as Shanghai and Sierra Leone, but always returned on leave to stay with Jack. When he retired from the army in 1932, he moved in with Jack and became his secretary. They lived together for the rest of their adult lives. Warnie began attending meetings of the Inklings and was encouraged to begin his own career as a writer. He eventually published seven books on French history.

During World War II, Warnie was briefly recalled to active duty. In his letters to Warnie, Jack described the first children who came to escape the dangers of wartime London, "I have said that the children are 'nice,' and so they are. But modern children are poor creatures. They keep . . . asking, 'What shall we do now?' . . . Shades of our childhood!" Different groups of children arrived throughout the war, and Warnie met many of them. We don't know exactly which ones gave Jack the idea for the premise for *The Lion, the Witch and the Wardrobe*. Perhaps it was more than one that asked about the old wardrobe.

Jack showed the first two chapters of *The Lion, the Witch and the Wardrobe* to J. R. R. Tolkien in 1949. Tolkien disliked them immensely. He thought that Lewis had not developed a consistent mythology to support the world of Narnia. Tolkien's disapproval of Lewis's children's stories and Hugo Dyson's dislike of Tolkien's *The Lord of the Rings* spelled the end of the friendly Inklings meetings.

Therefore Warnie's help as typist and first audience became crucial for The Chronicles of Narnia. When I visited the Kilns, the house outside Oxford where Warnie and Jack lived, I was struck by the old Royal typewriter. The tour guide informed us that C. S. Lewis never learned to type. He wrote all of his famous works for adults and children long-hand in exercise books with an old-fashioned fountain pen. He felt the noise of the typewriter prevented him from hearing the sounds of his words in his head. Jack liked the rhythm of stopping to dip his pen in ink, which helped him to think as he wrote. Warnie had learned to type in the army and he typed quite quickly although with just two fingers. For me, the old Royal typewriter became a symbol of their collaborative relationship and also of the differences between the two brothers that went back to their earliest childhood; a symbol of Jack's immersion in the world of imagination and of Warnie's more practical engagement with modern technology.

Warnie remained an integral part of Jack's life even after Jack met and became romantically involved with the American poet Joy Gresham. Jack married Joy when he was fifty-seven years old. Energetic, intellectual, and accomplished, Joy brought an unexpected grace to his life. By all accounts she got along well with Warnie, and he continued to live with them and to help Jack with his correspondence. When Joy tragically died of cancer a few years later, Warnie did his best to help Jack raise Joy's children. The brothers were bound together for life, first by the imaginary world of Boxen and then by Narnia.

The Chronicles of Narnia

There are seven books in The Chronicles of Narnia. C. S. Lewis originally published them in the following order:

1. *The Lion, the Witch and the Wardrobe* (1950)—In which the four Pevensie children discover Narnia and help Aslan undo the spell cast by the White Witch.
2. *Prince Caspian: The Return to Narnia* (1951)—In which the Pevensie children return to Narnia and join forces with Prince Caspian to defeat the evil Telmarines.
3. *The Voyage of the Dawn Treader* (1952)—In which the Pevensies are joined by their cousin Eustace and sail to the ends of the earth.
4. *The Silver Chair* (1953)—In which Eustace and his friend Jill escape from boarding school to Narnia where they find the missing Prince Rillian.
5. *The Horse and His Boy* (1954)—In which two boys and their horses save Archenland from the Calormen.
6. *The Magician's Nephew* (1955)—In which readers learn how Narnia came to be, how its animals came to have the gift of speech, and how the White Witch came to power.
7. *The Last Battle* (1956)—In which there is a conflict between true and false Narnians, and Aslan shows the Pevensie children the real paradise.

However, the order of the books is as follows if you are using the chronology of Narnian history:

1. *The Magician's Nephew*
2. *The Lion, the Witch and the Wardrobe*
3. *The Horse and His Boy*
4. *Prince Caspian: The Return to Narnia*
5. *The Voyage of the Dawn Treader*
6. *The Silver Chair*
7. *The Last Battle*

In which order should you read them? This question has puzzled publishers, scholars, and fans for decades. I would recommend that you begin with *The Lion, the Witch and the Wardrobe* because this book contains the best introduction for readers to the wardrobe, the world of Narnia, and the Pevensie children. The other books, even the prequel *The Magician's Nephew*, make more sense if you read *The Lion, the Witch and the Wardrobe* first.

Illustrator's Note

Though he eventually settled in England, C.S. Lewis never forgot the windswept landscapes of his childhood in Northern Ireland. Indeed, hints of Narnia seem to be around every bend there, from the lush, mossy forest parks to the ruins of castles clinging to cliffsides. I enjoyed immersing myself in C.S. Lewis's world and piecing together his life both in Ireland and in Oxford. The following historical details and research notes are worth mentioning:

Title page Jack and Warnie loved riding their bicycles over the Holywood Hills near their home of Little Lea. This view is pieced together from my own visit to the area, looking north toward Belfast Lough. While Belfast has grown, the views remain, for the most part, the same as in Jack's time.

By 1905 Jack would probably have worn a suit like his brother rather than the sailor suit popular for younger children, but I chose to use the clothes to differentiate the two boys.

1 Warnie went off to boarding school one month after the family moved into Little Lea, but the boys would have played together at home during school holidays. Little Lea today has a large addition on the left side.

2–3 Balder the Brave's costume is based on Arthur Rackham's illustrations in *Siegfried and the Twilight of the Gods* by Richard Wagner. The book kindled C.S. Lewis's interest in Norse mythology.

4–5 Jack was a very prolific and mature reader from an early age. I've included titles and authors that he enjoyed in his childhood: *Ben Hur, A Connecticut Yankee in King Arthur's Court*, H. G. Wells, *Gulliver's Travels, The Tale of Squirrel Nutkin* by Beatrix Potter. I've also included one of Jack's own first "books," a journal called "My Life."

Beside the chair is a little toy "garden" that Warnie made for his baby brother in 1901 in the lid of a biscuit tin. Later, Jack remembers this garden as his first glimpse of "paradise."

6 The castle in this image is loosely based on Dunluce Castle on the northern coast of Ireland, which Flora Lewis and the children visited in September of 1906. Some scholars think it may have influenced Lewis's descriptions of Cair Paravel.

7 We know from Jack and Warnie's "Boxen" writings that the characters in the childhood stories were men and animals dressed in suits. I chose to depict the boys as themselves rather than their characters so that they would be recognizable to the reader.

8–9 The original wardrobe was built by Jack's grandfather. It is darker in color than I have depicted here, but I tried to be true to the size and decoration of the original.

12 The boat by Jack's feet was a Christmas present in 1907, which may have been his model for the *Dawn Treader*. Warnie is contemplating one of his contributions to the world of Boxen: a steam ship called the HMS *Greyhound*.

13 I based these chairs on the Coronation Chair of England, which dates back to 1300. In attendance are many of the most memorable characters from Boxen.

14–15 The Mourne Mountains can be glimpsed from the countryside near Little Lea, though I have exaggerated their size here. (In truth the mountains are some thirty miles south of Belfast.) This view inspired Lewis's descriptions of Narnia with the mountains of Archenland beyond.

16 This boat is based on antique postcards of the *Duke of Connaught*, one of several ships in service from Belfast to Fleetwood from 1902 to 1930. It would have been an overnight voyage for the boys.

17 The school closed in 1910 and the abusive headmaster was committed to an insane asylum. The building has since been demolished.

18–19 In 1917 Jack fought in the trenches in the Somme valley. I based the background behind Warnie on war photographs of the ruined landscape near Beaucourt, France, in 1916.

20 Lewis describes imagining this view from his office window in the New Building, but since that room was inaccessible to me I chose to show the Cloisters building instead. It was a sunny spring day on my visit; no fauns or snow in sight.

22–23 Special thanks to Ty Rallens at The Kilns house in Oxford for answering my questions and providing extra resources to help with my research.

24–25 My thanks to Holy Trinity Church staff for allowing me to sit and sketch inside. Jack is not shown in his "usual" pew; he chose to sit to the left of the nearer pillar. Mrs. Moore and her daughter Maureen, who both lived with C. S. Lewis for many years, are shown in the row ahead of Jack.

26–27 The wardrobe was in a hallway beside the kitchen door. Missing from this image are books, which Jack and Warnie had piled all over the house. It is said that when C. S. Lewis died, there were more than five thousand books in the house.

34–35 This rock formation and view is inspired by Slieve Bearnagh, a peak in the Mourne Mountains that I climbed during my visit to Northern Ireland. It is a beautiful and haunting landscape; a fitting home for Aslan.

Bibliography

Carpenter, Humphrey. *The Inklings: C. S. Lewis, J. R. R. Tolkien, Charles Williams and their Friends.* London: HarperCollins, 2006.

Downing, David C. *Into the Wardrobe: C. S. Lewis and the Narnia Chronicles.* San Francisco: Jossey-Bass, 2005.

Gormley, Beatrice. *C. S. Lewis: The Man Behind Narnia.* Grand Rapids, Michigan: Eerdmans Books for Young Readers, 2005.

Heck, Joel D. "Warren Hamilton Lewis: His Brother's Brother." *The Chronicle of the Oxford University C. S. Lewis Society.* Vol. 6, no. 3 (October, 2009), 3–22.

Lewis, C. S. and W. H. Lewis. *Boxen: Childhood Chronicles Before Narnia.* London: HarperCollins, 2010.

Lewis, C. S. *Surprised by Joy: The Shape of My Early Life.* San Diego: Harcourt Brace Jovanovich, 1984.

Lewis, W. H. ed. *Letters of C. S. Lewis.* New York: Harcourt, Brace & World, Inc., 1966.

Poe, Harry Lee. *The Inklings of Oxford: C. S. Lewis, J. R. R. Tolkien, and Their Friends.* Grand Rapids, Michigan: Zondervan, 2009.

Ward, Michael. *Planet Narnia: The Seven Heavens in the Imagination of C. S. Lewis.* Oxford University Press, 2008.

Zaleski, Philip and Carol Zaleski. *The Fellowship: The Literary Lives of the Inklings: J. R. R. Tolkien, C. S. Lewis, Owen Barfield, and Charles Williams.* New York: Farrar, Straus and Giroux, 2015.

To my daughters, Abby and Allie, who have been my first and best readers and editors —C.M.
To Ed, who opened so many doors —J.L.

Text copyright © 2019 by Caroline McAlister
Illustrations copyright © 2019 by Jessica Lanan
Published by Roaring Brook Press
Roaring Brook Press is a division of Holtzbrinck Publishing Holdings Limited Partnership
120 Broadway, New York, NY 10271
mackids.com

Library of Congress Control Number: 2019932584

ISBN 978-1-62672-658-1

Our books may be purchased in bulk for promotional, educational, or business use.
Please contact your local bookseller or the Macmillan Corporate and Premium Sales Department
at (800) 221-7945 ext. 5442 or by email at MacmillanSpecialMarkets@macmillan.com.

First edition, 2019
Book design by Monique Sterling
Printed in China by RR Donnelly Asia Printing Solutions Ltd., Dongguan City, Guangdong Province

1 3 5 7 9 10 8 6 4 2

Wild Lands of the North

Great Falls

Lantern Waste

Ettinsmoor

River Shribble

Narnia

Aslan's How

Beruna

Cair Paravel

Galma

Terebinthia

Bight of Calormen

Anvard

Archenland

Winding Arrow River

Calormen   Dessert

Calormen

Tashbaan